DOMESTIC ARCHITECTURE IN RURAL FRANCE

BY SAMUEL CHAMBERLAIN

SKETCHES IN LITHOGRAPH, DRYPOINT, PENCIL AND WASH, OF SMALL CHÂTEAUX, FARMS, TOWN HOUSES, COTTAGES, MANOIRS, WINDMILLS, GATES, DOORWAYS, DETAILS, ETC.;
FROM
BURGUNDY, AUVERGNE, PROVENCE, NORMANDY, BRITTANY AND THE TOURAINE

ARCHITECTURAL BOOK PUBLISHING COMPANY, INC.,
New York, 10016

PLATES

Copyright © 1928, 1981 by Architectural Book Publishing Company, Inc.

Library of Congess Cataloging in Publication Data

Chamberlain, Samuel, 1895–1975. Domestic architecture in rural France.

Originally published: 1928.
1. Architecture, Domestic—France. 2. Architecture—Details. I. Title.
NA7346.C5 1981   728'.0944   81-7935
ISBN 0-8038-1578-6 (pbk.)   AACR2

Published simultaneously in Canada by Saunders of Toronto, Ltd., Don Mills, Ontario.
Printed in the United States of America

INTRODUCTION

Architecture has always attracted the artist. Samuel Chamberlain studied to be an architect, but instead became an artist whose lifetime concern was the portrayal of works of architecture. His long career as a draughtsman, etcher, and photographer began in the 1920s, after his first exposure during World War I to what is probably the most appealing countryside in western Europe—rural France, a mixture of centuries of both formal and domestic architecture set in a mellow and tended landscape that must have been a revelation to this young man raised on the latter-day frontier of the state of Washington.

He returned to France shortly after the war and his enthusiasm for pencil drawing occupied much of his time during his early travels when he explored the French provinces, happily drawing and sketching cottages and farmhouses, châteaux, *manoirs,* churches, and castles. This book, originally published in 1928 in a limited-edition portfolio, is reissued upon the urging of artists and architects who feel that the drawings should again be made available to students and professionals and, as well, to the many travelers who have special affection for the gentle beauty of the land of France.

Copying is the time-honored method for understanding a medium and discerning the problems of treatment for particular kinds of subject matter. Students working from these drawings by a master will learn what the pencil can do, and as a collection the drawings offer a wide range of challenging subjects that would not otherwise be readily available. The student, by alternately copying to develop technique and then drawing actual scenes from life to apply what he has learned, will begin to create his own work. By referring again to the Chamberlain drawings, he can soon become his own critic, discover his own mistakes, and practice constructively to correct them. Facility gained in this way is a valuable tool for achieving the ultimate goal, the student's informed, individual style.

These drawings can also abet a professional purpose in architectural rendering, as opposed to the freer objectives of the artist and sketcher. Architectural draughtsmen need to depict with great accuracy the details as well as the over-all effect of buildings; but it is important to train the hand and eye to give such drawings excitement and vitality. Using Chamberlain's sketches for exercises in free drawing will prove most helpful in adding life to the arbitrary requirements of architectural renderings.

This book will provide the amateur, too, with the pure pleasure of learning to sketch and of being able to report his travel experiences in a sketchbook full of drawings. It is important to remember that the whole purpose of sketching is to make an interesting drawing rather than a strictly realistic representation. In this connection, it is illuminating to compare the styles of Samuel Chamberlain and two of his contemporaries. John Taylor Arms was an extraordinary etcher whose talents permitted him to make drawings and prints of the most elaborate subjects in microscopic detail which were of great value as architectural studies. Louis Conrad Rosenberg, considered by many as one of the greatest delineators in the architectural field, was, on the other hand, known for his expression of the essence of a subject in few and telling lines.

Chamberlain had something of both of these approaches but also a different one of his own. He was known for the accuracy of his architectural detail and use of line, but especially for his magnificent portrayal of light and shade to create form, without over-burdening his drawing with minutia. How this was done is demonstrated here in his sketches and prints of complete structures of many styles and also in many charming details of doors, windows, chimneys, cornices, brickwork, masonry, wrought iron, and slate. Sinclair Hitchings, Keeper of Prints at the Boston Public Library, described this characteristic quality in his introduction to Chamberlain's autobiography, *Etched in Sunlight.* ". . . he has opened our eyes to our architectural heritage. As an artist, Chamberlain's fascination has been with light and line. He likes to see the world in full three-dimensional contrast of brightness and shadow. His pencil linear detail is sure and accurate, but does not attempt to be exhaustive. Light and contrast are used to suggest mass and relief. Choosing no little area of subject matter, he has gone far afield in pursuit of architectural landmarks, mighty and humble, of Europe and the United States."

Samuel Chamberlain attended the University of Washington, studied architecture at the Massachusetts Institute of Technology, received fellowships and many awards for his work as a graphic artist, and taught at the University of Michigan and at M.I.T. He published innumerable photographic books, and his drawings, dry points, and etchings have hung in major museums abroad as well as in this country. He was a member of the National Academy of Art and of the American Institute of Architects. A man of many talents, he was also a writer, book designer and collector, gourmet and traveler. His major work abroad was done in France, Italy, and Britain, and probably no one has observed the New England states as comprehensively as he did, both as printmaker and photographer. But his first love as an artist was France, which the nostalgic drawings and prints in this book amply show.

WALTER FRESE

FOREWORD

TO

"DOMESTIC ARCHITECTURE IN RURAL FRANCE"

FRANCE is not a country to be "done" hurriedly, save by lady buyers and Representatives of Congress studying "European conditions." Most architects in this pressing age unfortunately have to accelerate their travels whether they wish to or not. Who among them has not had to be content with a five seconds' glimpse of a fine old French country house through the smoky panes of a fast express? And who has not sworn softly at the circumstance, (it might be an impatient family or a hurried chauffeur), which forces one to pass by dozens of intriguing fragments of domestic architecture, with nothing better than scribbled notes or blurred snapshots to recall them.

One of the advantages of being an ambulant pencil pusher is that one is able to satisfy the repressions and the never-dormant "Wanderlust" of a thwarted architect.

This book has been prepared with the enthusiastic idea of collecting, in a painstaking and well-premeditated series of plates, examples of domestic architecture which a harassed architect might like to sketch, were his leisure unlimited and his encumberments nil. There being no urge to "get somewhere," it has been quite easy to stop by the roadside, pull out the portfolio, and make a sketch whenever a worthwhile subject came into view. A distinct effort has been made to dig up material from the hinterlands and crossroads, so that the risk of duplicating houses which have already been published might be reduced to a minimum.

Two sets of tires and many a pair of rubber heels were worn down in collecting this material, but it is needless to point out that the broad title of "Domestic Architecture in Rural France" does not intimate that the field has been completely covered. So rich is France in old houses that a five foot book shelf of such sketches would hardly exhaust it.

Some of these plates call for much more comment than others. The resumé which follows is given with the hope of providing a few interesting sidelights on some of the sketches.

Of all of the provinces of France, Normandy is indisputably the richest in material for a volume of this kind. Brittany and the other Northern departments seem barren beside it. Not as picturesque as Alsace, nor as grand geographically as Burgundy or Auvergne, and lacking the fabulous châteaux of the Loire, it remains, none the less, a Paradise for the architect. Therefore if a heavy percentage of these plates seem to spring from Normandy and the Eure, there is fair justification for the fact.

Half timber flourishes at its most, prodigal and flamboyant, in the neighborhood of Lisieux, the heart of Normandy. The countryside is dotted with a thousand forgotten manoirs and châteaux. Lisieux possesses some dizzy streets and many marvellous old houses, such as the Maison du Salamandre, which outgrotesque the most fantastic of Rouen's antiquities. Lisieux has been done to death, of course, but it revels in such a multitude of material that the five sketches on Plate 1 may reveal some new angles. The tipsy cafe is especially appropriate.

The tattered string of five houses, (Plate 2), is the most intriguing thing in the little unvisited town of Conches, which is lost in the hills of the Eure. Although occupied by several separate households, it does not lack unity. Built up of stone, with touches of brick and an afterthought of timber, it has a shabby roof of greenish grey slate, nonchalantly patched with unrelated bits of red tile. The house on the Rue St. Foy is probably the most unusual of the many timbered relics of the town.

The farm near Chartres, (Plate 3), said to date from the XIVth century, is a delightfully casual old place. The towers are grouped informally, like old ladies around a tea table. All three of the towers are inhabited, one by a flourishing family of pigs.

Vitré, "The Gateway of Brittany," is full of ingenious combinations of windows and doorways, (Plate 4), which might be adapted to small houses. The two facades from Dinan and Mennetou-sur-Cher observe nothing as rigid as an axis, yet they achieve a nice balance. The farmhouse door near Senlis once belonged to an old abbey. Window space adequate for a metropolitan shop is found in the facade at Gaillon. One has a furtive and shamefaced vision of "Ye Olde Hatte Shoppe" evolving along these lines.

Farmhouses become, after a while, a hobby for people with a passion for the antique. They are so unconscious of their charm, so free from artifice. A variety of timber treatment is noticeable in the three sagging veterans on Plate 5. The yard at Vernonnet is swarmed with carts and donkeys and browsing nags on market day, when the farmers come in to barter the week's growth of carrots and spinach, and to get the Saturday shave. In Emanville, the patched house is now used as a blacksmith's shop, but the towering old barn near Favrolles-la-Campagne still serves falteringly to house the Winter's supply of hay. One of the pleasantest farm-houses in the Eure is the Ferme des Fourneaux, near Vernonnet. The grizzled old farmer who owns it tells me that Claude Monet made sketches of it on two occasions. It is built around a court, the principal facade being embellished with a grotesquely distorted frieze of timberwork. The lithograph on Plate 10 shows the outer gateway to this fine old property, which slopes through mossy meadows to the banks of the Siene.

The timbered house on the outskirts of La Mailleraye-sur-Seine has an amusing elevation. New tile has replaced one of the thatched roofs, and the timbers are noticeably more loosely knit than is customary in Normandy. Bizy-Vernon is a dozing little village, very pastoral and unostentatious, overlooking the Seine. It abounds in sunny little corners such as the one shown on this plate.

Dinan belongs, without question, among the most picturesque towns of France. It combines a stern Breton hill town with a fantastic valley village nestling along the placid River Ronce. The view on Plate 8 is of the latter valley town, showing the beginning of that most bizarre of streets, the Rue de Jersual. The gay portal of the Ancien Hotel de Beaumanoir, (Plate 20), bobs up unexpectedly in the heart of this same town. Capering dolphins have been carved out of the flintiest of granite, to form the joyous balustrade which is reminiscent of a distant Salamanca or Avila. It is so perfectly preserved that it might have been carved yesterday. Two famous Breton houses are found in Dinan, shown in the lithograph on Plate 10. Both of them were porched houses at one time, but these shelters have long since been transformed into shops. The house on the left with the nightcap roof is particularly famous. It wobbles and totters but, being built of tremendous oak timbers, manages to evade the wreckers.

The rambling farmhouse near Macon, (Plate 9), incorporates the novel arrangement of setting back a portion of the principal facade some three feet behind the roof line. Shelter from the rain and a most interesting play of shadow is thus provided. The so-called chateau in Le Neubourg, a flourishing town in the grain-rich plains of the Eure, bears more resemblance to a weathered stone abbey. It is unsymmetrical to a startling degree, and one finds it difficult to follow a single axis to the ground. On a sunny market day it takes on an added dignity, looming up proud and calm above a seething mass of bartering bumpkins.

The little house in Vitré, partly converted into an epicerie, (Plate 11), and the strange timbered courtyard in Vernon are quite out of the ordinary. The proud axial emphasis given to the plumbing arrangements on the latter house are worthy of note if not of emulation.

Vernon is a simple, unpretentious town on the banks of the Seine, the railroad stop for the over-famed Giverny. There are a few exciting corners in Vernon, such as the glimpse of the church shown in the drypoint on Plate 12. The timbered house is not exceptional, dozens of similar ones being found in Rouen. The etching on Plate 52 gives some idea of the animation which grips the town's market place on a Saturday morning. The fountain in the foreground is quite a handsome affair, and one notes with some disillusionment that it is only a cast iron stock model, replicas of which appear in various town squares all over the country.

Mennetou-sur-Cher is a rather isolated village which, strangely enough, seems to be visited by a great many architects and illustrators. Once a fortified town, it still conserves four of its frowning gates, one of which adjoins the old timbered treasure on Plate 13. This house has been illustrated before, but it proved too irresistible to be left unsketched. The spacing of the doors and windows on the ground floor is most informal, and the combination overhead of timber and patterned brick, weathered and unrestored, is delightful.

France is so abundant with old cottages that subjects of the kind found on Plates 14 and 15 are easy to uncover. The task comes in picking the best ones and resisting the others. Possibly the most reposeful dwelling found on this entire expedition was the rhythmic bit of composition which lingers on a side road near Caudebec-en-Caux, (Plate 15). There is a melodic swing to this blending of house and hedge, culminating in just the proper flourish of bunched cedars. The other thatched cottages, one with an unaccustomed touch of hand-hewn clapboards, and the other equipped with an overhanging roof to protect the loft, possess much that would harmonize with the American countryside. The picket fence, so rare in France, seems to hint at the fact.

An interesting study of off-center balance and expressive window openings is found in the cheerful little chateau at St. Pierre-sur-Dives, (Plate 16). The entrance gate is not particularly good in design, but it does possess an intimate quality, with the crest of some fallen still clinging to it. Set in a verdant Springtime freshness of foliage, this little estate is very much of a bijou. A seemingly nameless hamlet on the wind-swept plateau north of Bayeux boasts the quite exceptional farm gate on this sheet. Few towns have as brilliant a natural situation as Avranches, overlooking the thorny, pale blue silhouette of Mont St-Michel, and fewer still have as dull an architectural aspect. It has this one charming corner on the market square, however. One has the evil-mindedness to picture this adapted as a triplex.

Stone, brick, stucco, timber, slate, thatch and even tin roofing were employed in the unostentatious old barn near Caudebec, (Plate 17). The two barns near Chartres belong to the same farm, but differ widely in character. The upper one, a mere skeleton, provides an accessible shelter for the farm wagons. One end serves to store hay, while the other is boxed in to keep the family Ford. The lower barn, a huge affair, houses the live stock. Its two unusual gables are honeycombed with the small square habitations of an army of pigeons. The owner of the farm proudly showed me a wall filled with diplomas and citations for his carrier pigeons which he trained for the French Intelligence Service during the war.

The handsome old house in Menilles, (Plate 18), is the residence of the village priests. It reposes behind impenetrable walls, and I had to use all of the wiles and persuasions of a tabloid reporter to be allowed to sketch it. The glorious buff patine on the plaster and the ripened tomato-red of the bricks give it much distinction of color. The roof tiles are slightly more orange in tone than the brick, and the shutters are a faded blue green. The lines of the farmhouse in Corneuil, (Eure), are certainly adaptable to many a suburban scene. It has seen better days, for now it serves as a village café and billiard parlor, and the massive wrought iron gates close upon a hoarse throng of wine-sprinkled peasants at every midnight closing hour.

In the neighboring village of Coudres is a farmyard with an area of at least two acres, enclosed by a wide assortment of buildings and walls, (Plate 19). Even a church is included in its voluminous boundaries. The main farm building is a beautifully balanced old mansion. Timber sprouts into use in a few of the minor buildings, but, on the whole, it is a symphony of brick and stucco. Details of what was probably the largest manure heap in the department of the Eure were more or less casually omitted from the foregrounds of these sketches.

A most exceptional bit of half timber work is the octagonal barn found in a misty meadow near La Bonneville. This is a most practical affair for housing animals in the manner of a locomotive roundhouse. The complexity of the interior timber work is terrific. The courtyard in Conches adds romance to a rather drab country hotel whose groceries are not so romantic.

It is a long jump, both geographically and architecturally, from here to the Mistral-swept plains of Provence and the quaint hill towns of the Cote d'Azur. Arles is better known for its Roman remains than for its houses, but an interesting example of the latter lurks on its outskirts, surrounded by funeral cedars and the leafless carcasses of a few sycamores, (Plate 22). The sunny farmhouse near Antibes once rested in seclusion along the shore line of the Mediterranean, but the hazards of civilization have placed a new motor highway at its very back door, and high-powered Hispano-Suizas roar past it at all hours. St. Raphael, once the simplest of fishing villages, has become chic and casinofied, but the old town remains intact, powdered with a glorious rose-colored dust. Four habitations, each with an exterior stairway of stone, are combined in the rambling old house in St. Raphael. One regrets that black and white can give no hint of its glorious, ripened color.

There is a severity about the house in Chateauneuf-en-Gadagne, (Plate 24), which is typical of Provence. The windows are sparse and well spaced, and the sadly shorn remnants of a classic doorway are visible on the ground floor. This little town, once a fortified stronghold, retains none of its past glory. Its streets are deserted, and goats roam speculatively over the grass-grown ruins of its feudal château. There is an unconscious charm to the house with barred windows in that artist's citadel, Cagnes-sur-Mer. The gaunt old farmhouse within gaping distance of the dramatic St. Paul-du-Var has something on the second floor which resembles a sleeping porch, but this cannot be. You probably are wondering where the windows are, and so am I. Maybe it once served as the county jail.

One of the prize finds of these wanderings is the old manoir on the flat coast near Mont St-Michel, (Plate 23). It is a most original bit of composition, and the decorative use of grey stone is capital. More of its amusing facade could have been shown, were it not for a disconcerting clump of bushes and several stacks of hay and twigs which cluttered up the foreground. The manoir near Ecos savors of the formality of the Rennaissance, yet it has a curious disdain for formal spacing. The two rounded elements, one of a romantic coop where you expect to find a blonde damsel cooing to her canary bird, the other which might be a varlet's retreat, are tied together by a graceful path of interest which centers at the main doorway. The facade is made barren by two blocked windows, doubtless mortared up to escape the dreaded window tax. Blanche de Castille once lived here, so one may be forgiven for forming fanciful thought about the place.

Plate 25 deals with two well known spots which have been immortalized by many an etcher and massacred by many a plump lady watercolorist. The twin houses in St. Lo are among the most remarkable in France, both because of their beautifully carved timbers and the unprecedented second story of unadorned stone. The bridge at Sospel, close to the Franco-Italian frontier, is infinitely picturesque, capped by a sun-burnt old gateway. A basket shop, a postcard stand and several whimpering tramps with outstretched palms find refuge under its roof.

The farmyard of the chateau near Senlis, (Plate 26), is much more charming than the formal of the chateau proper which adjoins it. The plump tower in the foreground is patched with battered brick in patterns which, doubtless, were once rigid and regular. The farmhouse on this plate is another topsy-turvy combination of materials and periods. The original house is the two-storied unit on the left, the facade most exposed to the rain being faced with brick and large blocks of sandstone. The roof is of tattered tile, and the timbers have been allowed to fade into a dullish black-brown.

Of the quartet of doorways on Plate 27, that of St. Trophime in Arles will prove most familiar. The doorway of the unusual old house in Lyons-le-Foret is pleasing in the ensemble, despite certain defects in design. This little town sprouts up lonesomely in the middle of a forest in the Eure, and is recommended as a perfect retreat for anyone seeking quiet seclusion. The dignity that belonged to Vitré in medieval times is reflected in the doorway from that town, one of the many to be found in roaming its streets. The doorway in Caudebec is noteworthy for the rare Gothic richness of the wood carving, which contrasts with the heavy bulk of the other timbers. They sag a bit, but still contrive to hold up a wobbly old house. The most unusual doorway, illustrated on Plate 46, is probably that from the renowned Rennaissance house in Beaume. It is composed of a rather squatty opening, surmounted by a richly carved lintel, above which is an oval window, heavily barred. The wooden doors of the little church door at St. Aubin are encrusted with the twelve apostles, all of whom have been neatly beheaded by the Revolutionists.

The highly picturesque brick and stone gateway to the vine-covered château near Honfleur, (Plate 28), belongs to that category of monument which the visiting school teacher from Iowa just can't believe is possible. The concierge's quarters above, enclosed with richly carved beams, are very homelike, and one envies her good fortune, despite rats and spiders. The farm building near Pont-Audemer is much less ancient. It is clear that the masons and bricklayers had a perfectly swell time when they built this. It seems to be a joyous, loud-mouthed, race-tracky sort of place, and one can picture it ideally adapted as a hard drinking Hunt Club. Verneuil, one of the most classic sites in Normandy, is the fortunate possessor of several houses similar to the one here illustrated. The checkerboard pattern of brick and stone is, in reality, quite subdued and restful, and the corner tower is a beautifully detailed bit. The stone carving has been preserved with hardly a moss mark.

Though not actually in Brittany, the quaint cross-roads corner near Vire, (Plate 29), is entirely Breton in feeling, resplendent with flat slabs of stone and wide chimneys. There is a restaurant, a café and tobacco store, a grocery store and a dry goods merchant all on this picture. What more can one ask? The Manoir de Préaux, on the same sheet, is a gaunt, chateau-like structure, ripened and harmless with age, in an inconspicuous little town between Orbec and Livarot.

The essence of Springtime in Normandy seems to be found in the squatty little cottages, veiled by a screen of slendor saplings, at Notre-Dame de Bliquetuit. It is safe to hazard the guess that the two buildings must have been one at some time. The stark and skeletony timbers of the Maison Normande at La Mailleraye afford a study of a comparatively rare type of timbered house.

The low, rambling lines and casual window openings of the house in the hills near Le Puy, (Plate 31), could be adapted with small difficulty to a contemporary country house. This is a stern country, and the courageous farmers who try to eke a living out of the barren soil are rare indeed. Rock and slate are abundant, and rarely does one observe a house, such as this, surfaced with stucco instead of the bare stone. The lump of three widely different houses at Tinquerville, flanked by the bulk of the village church and an enormous chestnut tree, makes up a pleasing composition, even though none of the houses has any pronounced interest. The small château near Lisieux was found slumbering in a cool meadow one misty Spring morning, which accounts for the greyness of the sketch. It has a whimsy of stone and brick texture which harmonizes with the soft delicacy of a screen of soaring poplars in the distance and the quivering reflections of a lily-spotted moat. On closer inspection, the whole structure is found to be covered with a pleasant mottle of lichens.

It is a bit perplexing to figure out a raison d'etre for a certain type of farmhouse found in Burgundy, illustrated in the central sketch on Plate 32. The same type is found in the dreary stretches of the Champagne. The roofs are not well formed to best withstand the heavy snows which visit the region. However, it is a very compact arrangement, admirable indeed, if you care to sleep under the same roof with the horses and cattle. The genial cultivator informed me that the biggest part of the house was underground. It consists of an expansive wine cave, filled with maturing kegs of red Burgandy. Timbered houses are scarce in that butter-and-egg sector of France known as the Jura, which gives the old farm near Dole a particular interest. The heavy overhang of the roof and the two exterior stairways are equally unique. The barn door is enormous.

A considerable amount of elimination was practised in selecting the shop signs and fragments of wrought iron on Plate 33. Even so, many of them lack purity of design, but they compensate for this with their individuality. All of them are ancient, I believe, save the two details from Jumiéges, (which embellish the gates that bar hopeful artists from sketching the Abbaye), the keysmith's sign in Colmar (his own work), and the sign on the pharmacist's shop in the same city, which is the work of the celebrated artist and French patriot, Hansi. Two of the other pieces have come from Italy.

Saumur, on the broad banks of the Loire, is one of the classic towns of France. Hardly a cottage can be found here unembellished with a set of carefully chiselled mouldings. There is a needle-shaped island in the middle of the river, on which linger the celebrated Gothic residence of the Queen of Sicily, now sadly turned into powdered limestone, and the charming domestic duo shown at the bottom of Plate 34. Touches of timber relieve the monotony of stained stone surface. The roofs are slipshod and tatterdemalion.

The famous house of the Kings of France, (Plate 35), once boasted much more splendor than it can claim at the present sad moment. Twenty years ago the major portion of its imposing mass was torn away to make room for a modern monstrosity of gee-gaw architecture which houses the Caisse d'Epargne. The courtyard which once received the noblest of Saumur's visitors is now littered with the junk of a second hand furniture dealer, who has erected a frightful shelter for his ragged merchandise. Only the tower, reminiscent of a movie set, remains relatively undamaged. Many a prisoner has languished therein, according to the venerable caretaker who roosts there now.

The country grocery store in Bourg-en-Bresse, (Plate 36), could be duplicated a thousand times in the French countryside, and the squat house which contains it can claim no other distinction than being typical of hundreds of others. Quite the contrary may be said of the little fragment from the time of François Ier on the same plate. This surely boasted a different roof in the days of its prime, and probably did not have its corners sliced away as they are at present. The carving on the two upper windows remains unblemished, and one wonders what sort of window or doorway graced the area now occupied by a discordant shop front. The slouching timbered house on the right is not exaggerated, and it looks as though its ultimate collapse can be but a matter of minutes. But the timbers which hold its sinews together are enormous, and possibly my grandchildren will pass by some day and observe the same house staggering in the same ancient fashion, still housing a family of screaming washwomen.

Alsace provides an entirely different aspect of La Belle France, bearing small resemblance, architecturally speaking, to the rest of the country. The weathered old house in Aspach-le-Bas, (Plate 37), a coy village on the verge of the boundary line which once separated German Alsace and France, expresses this individuality. Yet there is something about it, strangely enough, which convinces one that it would sink pleasantly into the American rural scene. The picket fence, the sheathing of slate on the rain-exposed wall and the wooden shutters with diamond-shaped cut-outs all have a certain familiarity. The vast frame of one of Colmar's oldest Gothic houses is encrusted with the mad jumble of doorways, windows and details shown on this plate. The pointed window on the left for years served to provide light for the lurid brush of the master Schongauer. The ensemble is far more commendable as a study of detail than as a composition. Three houses of different shape rarely cluster together so homogeneously as they do in the group at Cernay, (Plate 38). It is interesting to note the loose-jointed assembling of Alsatian timber work and the relative equality between the vertical and horizontal members, with the diagonal ones coming in a close third. Nothing is more characteristic of Alsace, save snub-nosed roofs. There is a touch of fantasy to the house in Guémar and its plump little tower, which is roofed with an inexplicable pattern of tiles. The whole thing lurks behind a hedge of shrubs and a pair of ferocious watch dogs, and I could invade the privacy of the precincts no farther than is indicated. The three villages of Ammerschwihr, Kaysersberg and Riquewihr, although more famous for their wines than for architecture, are among the most incredibly picturesque in France, though these sketches but faintly attest to the fact.

The principal examples of Breton stonework on Plate 39 come from the delightful Josselin, in the mathematical heart of Brittany. There are many unique structures here, among them the celebrated Maison d'Ovys Pichelin, whose timbered eccentricities bear an astonishing resemblance to the old houses of Herefordshire. The cottage whose herringbone timbers are framed in stonework is extremely rare. On the contrary, the stone doorway at Dol is typical of hundreds of others. The Large XVIth century house with the stone well has a half dozen counterparts of equal charm in Josselin.

The temperamental river Loire has for centuries been walled with an embankment which stretches, in the form of an elevated roadway, all the way from Blois to Angers. There has resulted a distinct type of house, huddling against these dike-like embankments for protection against the sweeping river winds. The facade is usually a low, one story affair, (Plate 40), resting on the road level, while the rear elevation shows two complete floors and a well developed attic. The farm house near Beaune, on this plate, is mainly intriguing for its exterior stairways, and the cottages near La Fleche and Cinq Mars both boast highly amusing roof lines.

Since old wrought iron has become the prey of collectors and antique dealers, it has been increasingly difficult to uncover good and unusual examples on a sketching trip. One is almost forced to haunt the museums for the most exceptional examples. Most of the material presented in Plates 41, 42 and 53 is in the collections of the Cluny Museum, Paris, and the Victoria and Albert Museum, South Kensington.

One can afford to overwork a few superlatives in speaking of the magnificent Manoir d'Ango near Dieppe, (Plate 43). There may be a more perfect and impressive manor house in France, but I have never been able to find trace of it, either in books or in the countryside itself. The manor is built entirely around a vast square court, on the central axis of which is a round tower for storing grain, a most astounding bit of brickwork. There is a dearth of trees on the estate, particularly in the courtyard, but, aside from this, the Manoir d'Ango comes as near being romantic perfection as anything one could hope to find. The stone carving is subtle and suave, the wall textures have an extraordinary interest and the timberwork possesses an almost exotic originality. Visitors to Dieppe were not long in discovering its charm, and now it has been restored, with remarkable fidelity to the original, and converted into a hostelry for those who appreciate its magnificence. The historic old Ferme de la Touche, (Plate 44), built around a court also, cannot claim the same splendor as the Manoir d'Ango, but its profile is quite as engaging. The lines of the vast barn near Douains are so simple that the sense of enormity of the place is almost lost until a farm wagon or a human figure enters upon the scene to lend scale. The combined barn and wagon shelter on this plate is one of a number of buildings belonging to a prosperous farmer in the Eure. Its lines are graceful, even though a tractor has been appended to one extremity. The hired hands sleep in the attic.

The mild feudalism of the Touraine in the good old days is well expressed in the entrance gate of a small château which lurks in a lost meadow near Montrichard, (Plate 45). The handsome central tower and the well proportioned lines of the roof, silhouetted against the black-green of gigantic chestnuts, are much more interesting than the château itself. The rounded towers and grotesque roof lines of the château-farm near St. Calais are unconventional yet imposing. The entrance of the long ruined Château de Blerancourt, so dear to the heart of The American Committee for Devastated France, combines a concierge's lodge on either bay with a rich archway. In the distance is a stone gate of the same epoch, a thing of great richness and beauty of design.

The stone manor on the outskirts of Bayeux, (Plate 47), now serves as a simple farmhouse, but must, at one time, have been a lordly estate. The treatment of the chimneys and the triple-arched stables are worthy of note. The château near Doué-la-Fontaine, in addition to its towers and turrets and richly detailed doorways, has a splendid moat which this sketch fails to reveal. The Château de Grandchamp, (Plate 48), is one of the treasures of Normandy which has recently been restored by an appreciative purchaser. The fragments here shown have been converted into a garage and chauffeur's living quarters. The rambling old Manor on the banks of the Loire could spring up nowhere but in the Touraine, nor would the flat lines of the Château de la Pioline, framed in giant plaine trees, seem at home outside of Provence.

There is an intimate, small town atmosphere about the town gate in Amboise, (Plate 49), which, by stretching a point, almost places it in the category of domestic architecture. The stone has aged into a multi-colored grey and the roof glistens with the soft blue of weathered slate.

There crop up, in protracted wanderings such as were occasioned in preparing this volume, a quantity of smaller subjects, interesting in one way or another, yet not meriting a large sketch. A good many of these have been collected in the three plates, Nos. 50, 51 and 55. Some of them were sketched merely because they looked like good fun and were too irresistable to be missed.

The domestic application of windmills, (Plate 54), is a bit vague in the author's mind, but, being the most dramatic bits of unpretentious architecture left standing in France, they proved too sketchable to be omitted. Windmills do not prosper in France in this advanced day, but a few survivors still manage to pump enough water to justify their existence. When their wings cease to turn, they still retain utility as store houses for grain or fodder. The mill near Romarantin has actually been adapted as a workshop and living quarters by an imaginative farm mechanic.

Such is a flighty resumé of some of the material uncovered on this extended sketching tour. I could recount further details and adventures, such as the time my coat tails caught fire in a dark doorway, or when I drove blandly into a ditch while gazing backwards at an intriguing cottage, or the numerous occasions upon which I have been mistaken for a bill poster, an itinerant photographer and a wall paper salesman. The campstool sketcher's exposure to the hospitality of conversational Frenchmen has resulted in many friendships and literally hundreds of "petits verres" in the nearest café. More than one flattered proprietor of a sketchable house has, upon hearing my Amurrican "r", endeavored to sell it to me.

I confess to recalling certain sublime platters of "Poulet a la Valée d'Auge" more vividly than some of these Normandy manoirs, and a few aged bottles of Gévrey-Chambertin remain more affectionately imprinted on my mind than many of the farmhouses of Burgundy.

Now, at the conclusion of these travels, I am seriously considering the preparation of three volumes entitled, "A Gastronomic Manual for Unsuspecting Guests of Village Inns," "How to Hypnotize Watchdogs" and "Grouchy Garagists I Have Known." I don't know which one to begin first.

SAMUEL CHAMBERLAIN.

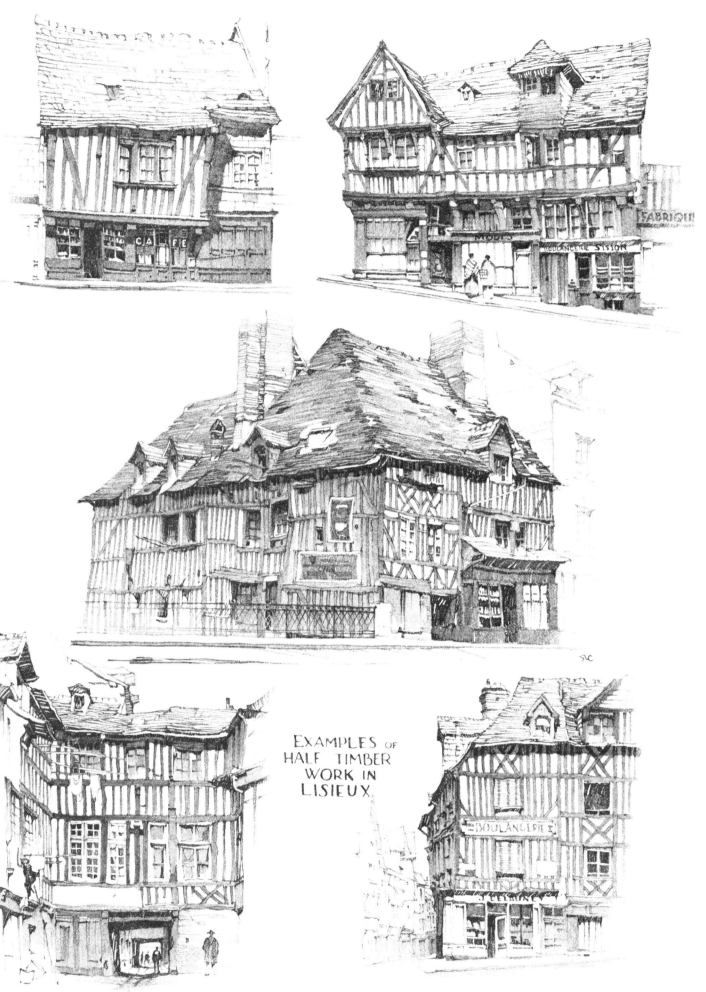

EXAMPLES OF
HALF TIMBER
WORK IN
LISIEUX

Plate I

A String of Small Houses

Architectural Fragments from Conches (Eure)

EPICERIE

A Grocery Store

Detail of the Hotel de Ville

CAFE Ste FOY

Houses on the Rue Ste Foy

Plate II

AN OLD FARM NEAR CHARTRES

Plate III

DETAIL OF A HOUSE IN VITRE

HOUSE IN VITRÉ

DETAILS

FACADE OF THE GROUND
FLOOR OF A HOUSE ON THE
RUE DE JERSUAL DINAN

DETAIL OF A HOUSE
IN MENNETOU·SUR·CHER

DOORWAY OF A
FARMHOUSE NEAR
SENLIS

FACADE IN GAILLON

Plate IV

A FARMHOUSE IN VERNONNET

FARMHOUSES.

F MANVILLE

NEAR FAVEROLLES-LA-CAMPAGNE

Plate V

EAST WING

FARMYARD OF MONSIEUR BILLEBOT
FERME DES FOURNEAUX
VERNON

WEST WING

NORTH WING

Plate VI

TIMBERED HOUSE
ON THE OUTSKIRTS OF LAMAILLERAYE-SUR-SEINE

ELEVATION

BIZY VERNON

Plate VII

Plate VIII

THE CHATEAU - LE NEUBOURG

FARMHOUSE NEAR MACON

Plate IX

The Farm Gate

CAFE
PORCHES

Dinan

Plate X

TIMBERED HOUSE IN THE COURTYARD OF
THE CAFE DES TROIS MARCHANDS - VERNON

HOUSE IN VITRE

Plate XI

THE WINDING ROAD — VERNON

Plate XII

SIXTEENTH CENTURY
HOUSE IN
MENNETOU-sur-CHER

A GATEWAY IN MENNETOU SUR CHER

Plate XIII

COTTAGES.

COTTAGE BEHIND WALLS IN VERNONNET

COUDRES.

SMALL HOUSE IN LA MAILLERAYE

RESTORED FARMHOUSE IN BIZY (EURE)

NEAR PACY·SUR·EURE

LOUVERSEY

TWO COTTAGES IN CROISY

Plate XIV

House near Caudebec-en-Caux

Three Thatched Cottages
in Normandy

Cottage near Pacy-sur-Eure

Cottage near Jumieges

Plate XV

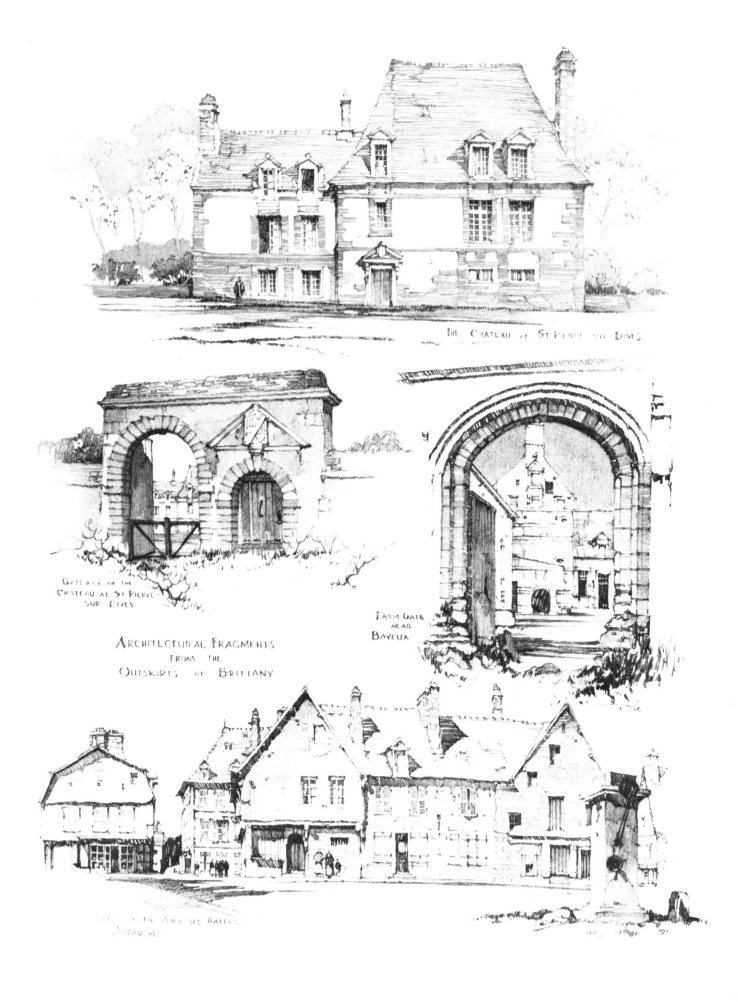

The Chateau at St Pierre sur Dives

Gateway of the Chateau at St Pierre sur Dives

Farm Gate near Bayeux

ARCHITECTURAL FRAGMENTS
FROM THE
OUTSKIRTS OF BRITTANY

Houses in the Place des Halles, Avranches

Plate XVI

Barn Buildings

Barn on the Outskirts of Caudebec-en-Caux

Barn near Chartres

Farmhouses in Picardy

Another Barn near Chartres

Plate XVII

TWO HOUSES IN THE EURE

18TH CENTURY HOUSE IN
MENILLES

FARMHOUSE IN CORNEUIL (EURE)

Plate XVIII

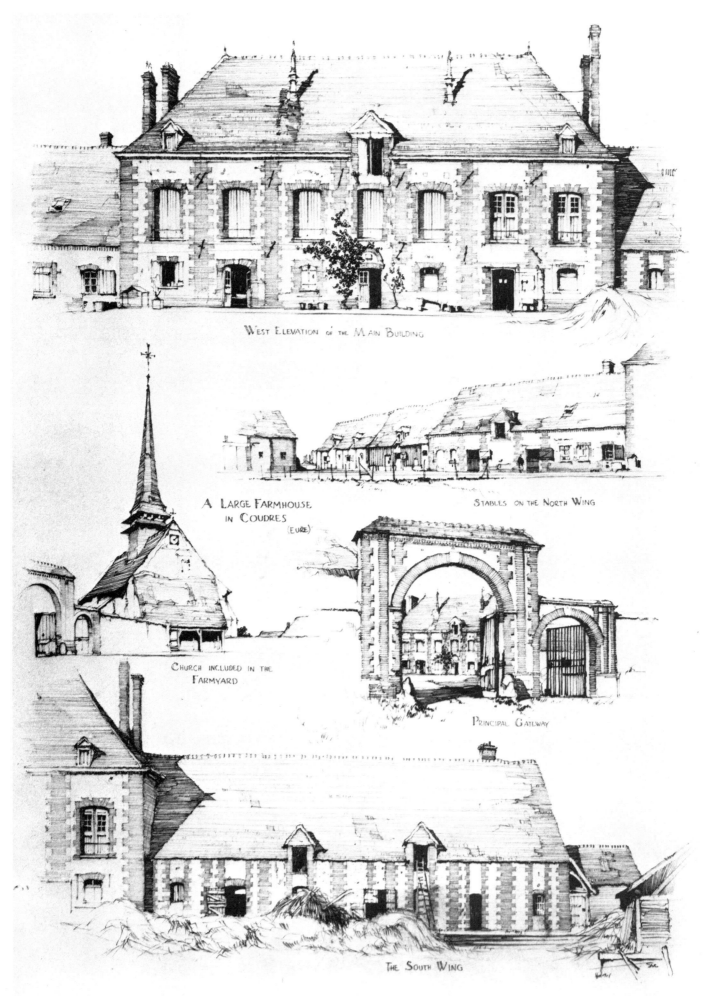

West Elevation of the Main Building

Stables on the North Wing

A Large Farmhouse
in Coudres
(Eure)

Church included in the
Farmyard

Principal Gateway

The South Wing

Plate XIX

DOORWAY OF THE
ANCIEN HOTEL DE BEAUMANOIR · DINAN

Plate XX

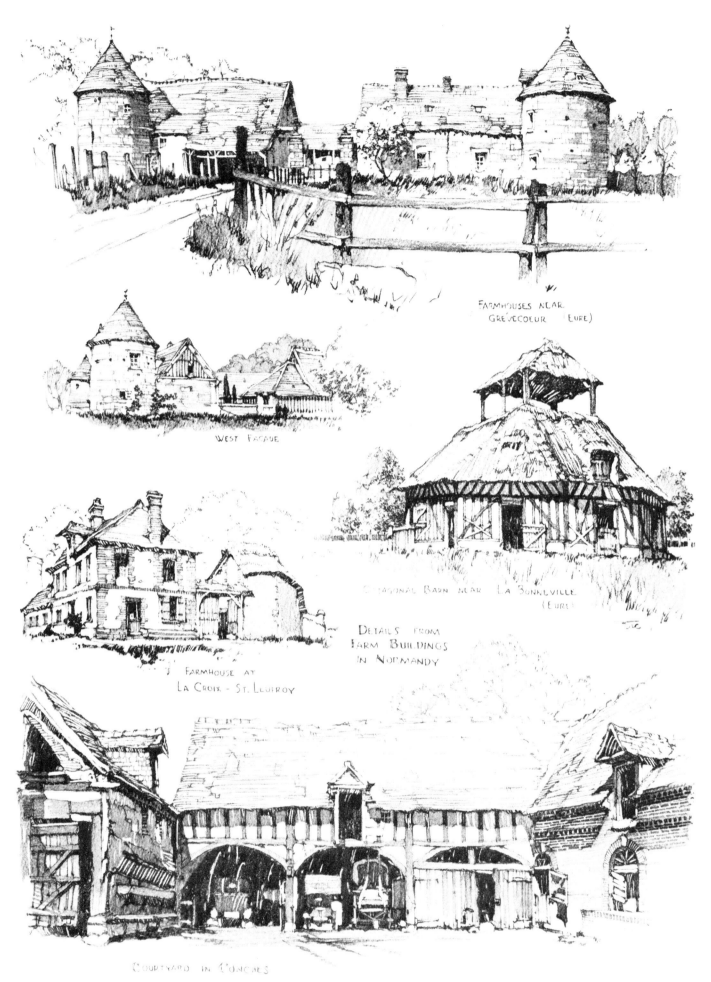

FARMHOUSES NEAR
GRÈVECOEUR (EURE)

WEST FACADE

OCTAGONAL BARN NEAR LA BONNEVILLE
(EURE)

DETAILS FROM
FARM BUILDINGS
IN NORMANDY

FARMHOUSE AT
LA CROIX - ST. LEUFROY

COURTYARD IN CONCHES

Plate XXI

FARMHOUSE OUTSIDE OF ARLES

RENNAISCANCE HOUSE IN LES BAUX

THE LIPTON

FARMHOUSE NEAR ANTIBES

PROVENÇAL HOUSES

COURTYARD IN ST RAPHAEL

Plate XXII

MANOIR NEAR
MONT ST-MICHEL

BACK VIEW

MANOIRS

CHAUSSY

MANOIR NEAR ECOS (EURE)

Plate XXIII

HOUSE AT CHATEAUNEUF-DU-GADAGNE

THREE HOUSES IN PROVENÇAL HILL TOWNS

HOUSE IN CAGNES SUR MER

FARMHOUSE AT ST. PAUL-DU-VAR

Plate XXIV

Plate XXV

FARMHOUSE NEAR
ELBEUF

FARMYARD OF A CHÂTEAU
NEAR SENLIS

Plate XXVI

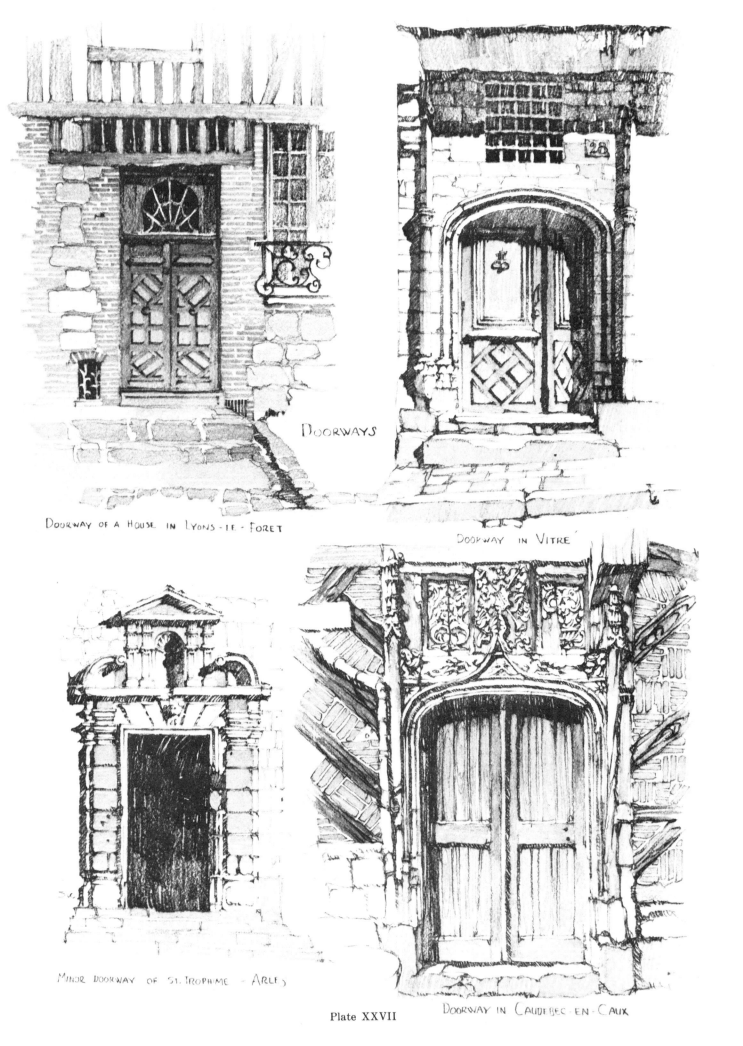

DOORWAYS

DOORWAY OF A HOUSE IN LYONS-LE-FORET

DOORWAY IN VITRE

MINOR DOORWAY OF ST. TROPHIME - ARLES

DOORWAY IN CAUDEBEC-EN-CAUX

Plate XXVII

DETAIL FROM LA MAILLERAYE SUR SEINE

STONE AND BRICK COMBINATIONS

DOORWAY IN QUILLEBOEUF

ENTRANCE GATEWAY OF A SMALL CHATEAU NEAR HONFLEUR

FARM BUILDING NEAR PONT-AUDEMER

HOUSE IN VERNEUIL

Plate XXVIII

MANOIR IN PRÉAUX

CROSSROAD NEAR VIRE

Plate XXIX

COTTAGE IN
NOTRE-DAME DE BLIQUETUIT

MAISON NORMANDE — LA MAILLERAYE SUR SEINE

Plate XXX

COUNTRY HOUSES

HOUSE IN THE HILLS OF AUVERGNE NEAR LE PUY

GROUP OF HOUSES IN TINQUERVILLE

SMALL CHATEAU NEAR LISIEUX

Plate XXXI

FARMHOUSE
NEAR BELFORT

TYPICAL FARMHOUSE IN BURGUNDY   NEAR BEAUNE

FARMHOUSES FROM CENTRAL FRANCE

FARMHOUSE OF THE JURA
NEAR DOLE

Plate XXXII

BRACKET FROM THE
AUBERGE DU VIEUX PUITS
PONT-AUDEMER

BRACKET IN NICE

WEATHER VANE FROM A
CHURCH IN THE OLD QUARTER
OF NICE

BRACKET IN
LA CROIX - ST. LEUFROY (EURE)

DETAIL FROM THE ANCIENNE
DOUANE - COLMAR

DETAILS FROM THE ANCIENNE DOUANE - COLMAR

Metz Freres

KEYSMITH'S SHOP
SIGN IN COLMAR

FROM A WINDOW GRILLE IN COLMAR

SIGN ON A
PHARMACIST'S
SHOP IN COLMAR

SCATTERED
FRAGMENTS
OF
IRONWORK

LANTERN BRACKET
IN JUMIÈGES

ITALIAN
BRACKET FROM
AN ANTIQUE SHOP
IN MENTON

DETAIL FROM JUMIÈGES

DETAIL FROM Nº 20
RUE DES SAINTS PERES
PARIS

BRACKET FROM THE
MUSÉE SCHONGAUER - COLMAR

Plate XXXIII

HOUSE ON THE BANK OF THE LOIRE
SAUMUR

HOUSES IN SAUMUR

SAUMUR

HOUSES ON THE
FAUBOURG · DES · PONTS
SAUMUR

Plate XXXIV

HOUSE OF THE KINGS OF FRANCE – SAUMUR

Plate XXXV

OLD HOUSES IN BOURG-EN-BRESSE

BOURG-EN-BRESSE

Plate XXXVI

HOUSE IN ASPACH-LE-BAS
(ALSACE)

THE STUDIO OF SCHONGAUER - COLMAR

Plate XXXVII

HOUSES IN CERNAY (ALSACE)

CERNAY

HOUSE IN GUEMAR

A CHATEAU IN GUEMAR

ALSATIAN SKETCHES.

AMMERSCHWIHR

KAYSAHR

Plate XXXVIII

BRETON STONEWORK

DOUBLE DOORWAY OF THE
MAISON DOUYS YICHELIN · JOSSELIN

COTTAGE IN
JOSSELIN

DOORWAY AT DOL

WINDOW IN QUIMPERLE

FARM GATE
NEAR
LANDIVISEAU

16TH CENTURY HOUSE IN JOSSELIN

Plate XXXIX

HOUSE ON THE BANKS OF THE LOIRE
NEAR LANGEAIS

SMALL HOUSES

FARMHOUSE NEAR BEAUNE

ON THE OUTSKIRTS OF LA FLECHE

NEAR
CINQ MARS

Plate XL

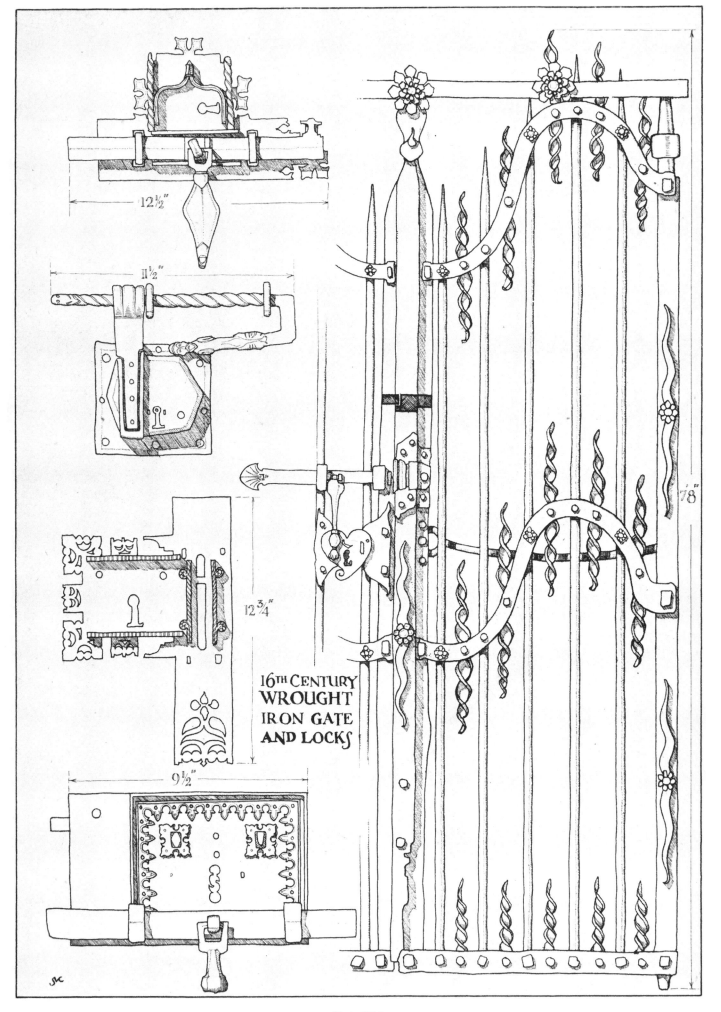

12½"

11½"

12¾"

9½"

16TH CENTURY
WROUGHT
IRON GATE
AND LOCKS

78"

Plate XLI

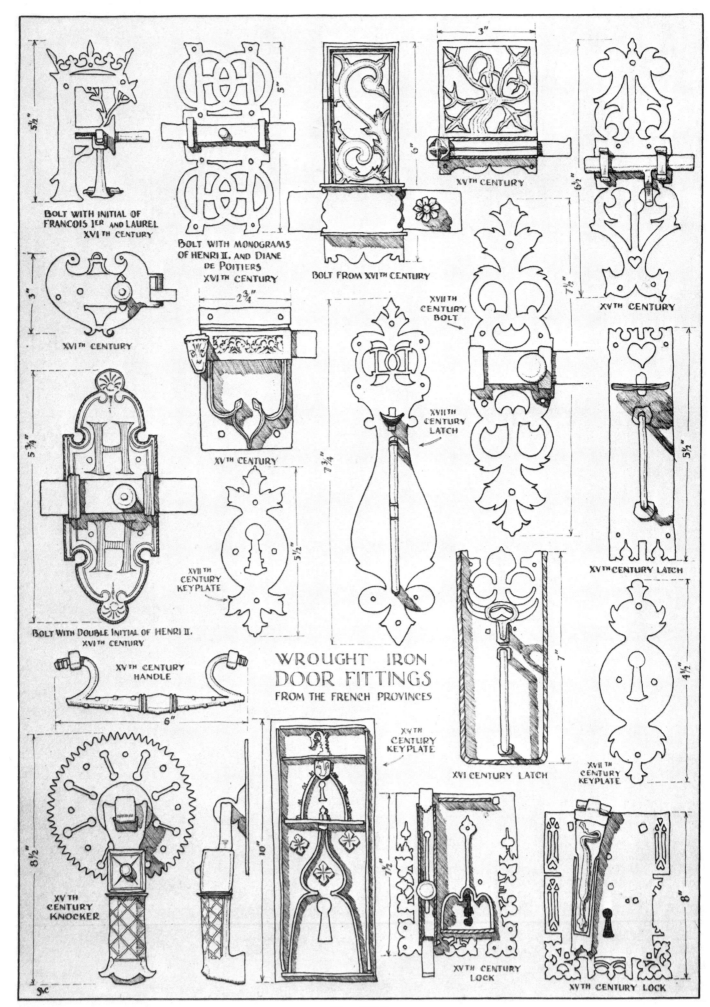

BOLT WITH INITIAL OF
FRANCOIS 1ER AND LAUREL
XVITH CENTURY

BOLT WITH MONOGRAMS
OF HENRI II. AND DIANE
DE POITIERS
XVITH CENTURY

BOLT FROM XVITH CENTURY

XVTH CENTURY

XVTH CENTURY

XVITH CENTURY

XVTH CENTURY

XVIITH
CENTURY BOLT

XVIITH
CENTURY
LATCH

XVIITH
CENTURY
KEYPLATE

BOLT WITH DOUBLE INITIAL OF HENRI II.
XVITH CENTURY

XVTH CENTURY
HANDLE

XVTH CENTURY LATCH

XVITH CENTURY
KEYPLATE

XV
CENTURY
KEYPLATE

XVI CENTURY LATCH

WROUGHT IRON
DOOR FITTINGS
FROM THE FRENCH PROVINCES

XV TH
CENTURY
KNOCKER

XVTH CENTURY
LOCK

XVTH CENTURY LOCK

Plate XLII

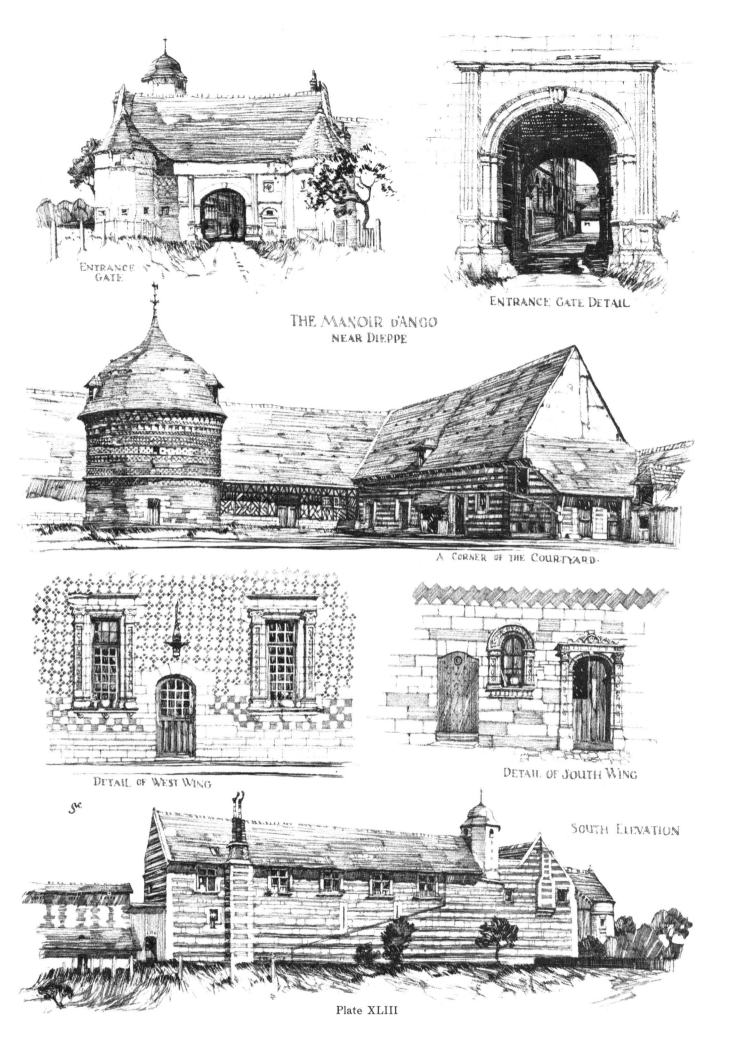

ENTRANCE GATE

ENTRANCE GATE DETAIL

THE MANOIR D'ANGO
NEAR DIEPPE

A CORNER OF THE COURTYARD.

DETAIL OF WEST WING

DETAIL OF SOUTH WING

SOUTH ELEVATION

Plate XLIII

Ferme de la Touche   near Doue la Fontaine

Farm Buildings.

Barn at Douains

Barn and Wagon Shelter — Favrolles

Plate XLIV

ENTRANCE GATE OF A
CHÂTEAU near MONTRICHARD

CHÂTEAU ENTRANCES

CHÂTEAU GATES AND
FARM BUILDINGS near
ST. CALAIS

ENTRANCE TO THE CHÂTEAU DE BLÉRANCOURT   (AISNE)

Plate XLV

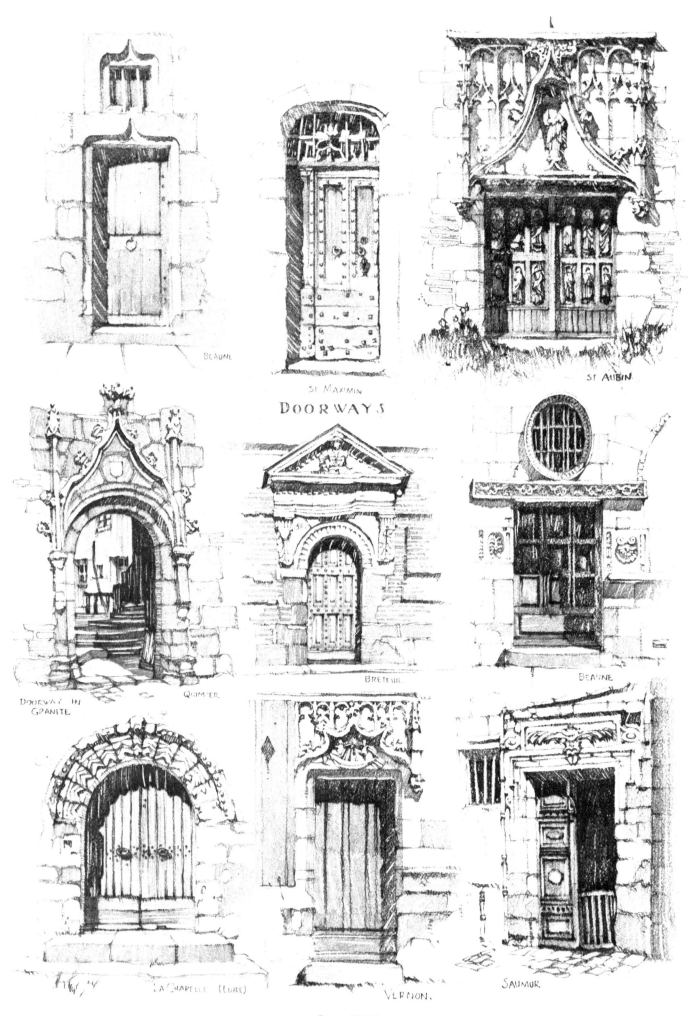

BEAUNE

ST MAXIMIN

ST AUBIN

DOORWAYS

DOORWAY IN GRANITE   QUIMPER

BRETEUIL

BEAUNE

LA CHAPELLE (EURE)

VERNON.

SAUMUR

Plate XLVI

MANOIR ON THE OUTSKIRTS OF BAYEUX

SMALL CHÂTEAUX

DOVE COTE
NEAR TOURS

A CORNER OF THE COURTYARD OF THE MANOIR NEAR BAYEUX

SMALL CHÂTEAU NEAR
DOUE-LA-FONTAINE

Plate XLVII

ENTRANCE GATE AND STABLES
CHATEAU DE GRANDCHAMP

CHATEAUX FROM NORMANDY,
THE TOURAINE AND PROVENCE

XVI.ᵀᴴ CENTURY MANOIR NEAR TOURS

CHATEAU DE LA POLINE - VAUCLUSE

Plate XLVIII

THE TOWN GATE   AMBOISE

Plate XLIX

HOUSE ON THE ROUTE DES QUARANTE SOUS NEAR CAEN

FARMHOUSE NEAR AIX-EN-PROVENCE

NEAR ST BRIUC

CHATEAU FARM NEAR ST GILLES (PROVENCE)

THUMBNAIL SKETCHES

MENILLES

AN ARTISTS HOUSE NEAR ACQUIGNY

FARM NEAR PONT L'EVEQUE

FARMHOUSE NEAR BRIGNOLES PROVENCE

CROSSROADS NEAR LISIEUX

FARM NEAR BOURG-EN-BRESSE

MANOIR NEAR GRANDCHAMP

ENTRANCE GATES OF THE CHATEAU DE MONTICEL

Plate L

THUMBNAIL
SKETCHES
(II)

ANGERS

COLMAR

P 62

FARMHOUSE NEAR ST ANDRE

DESERTED COTTAGE
NEAR PONT L'EVEQUE

CORNER OF A FARMYARD
NEAR COMPIEGNE

GATEWAY AT ISSENHEIM
(ALSACE)

WELL AT LE NEUBOURG

FARMHOUSE NEAR BELFORT

HOUSE IN LANDIVISEAU (BRITTANY)

HOUSE ON THE
RIVERBANK
BESANCON

ABANDONNED HOUSE
NEAR EVREUX

FARM BUILDINGS NEAR IVRY (EURE)

FARMHOUSE NEAR CHINON

Plate LI

The Market Place - Vernon

Plate LII

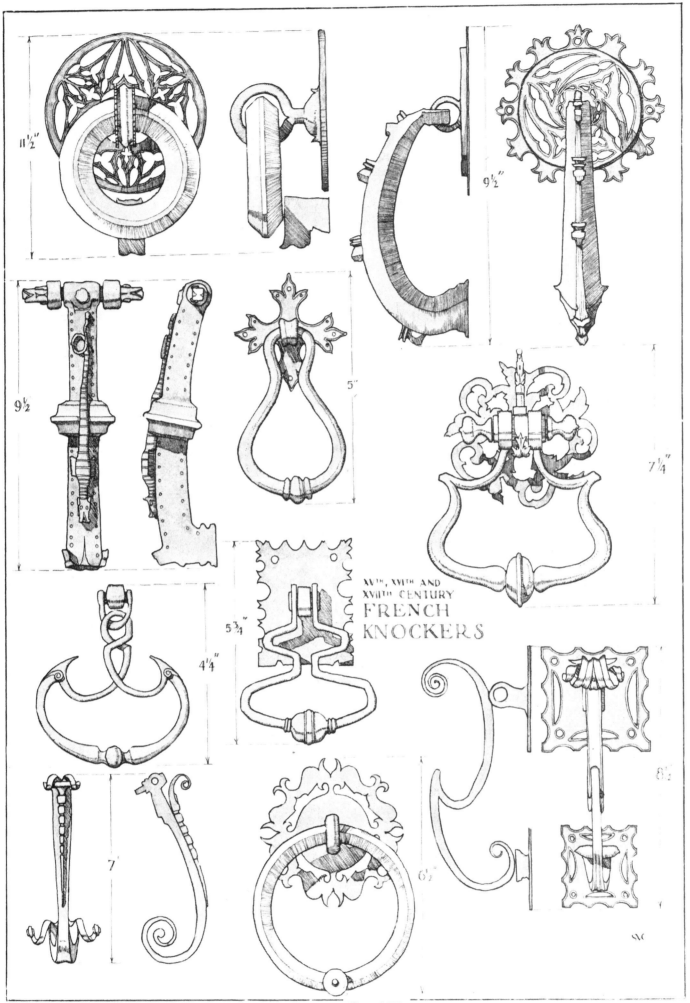

XV TH, XVI TH AND
XVII TH CENTURY
FRENCH
KNOCKERS

Plate LIII

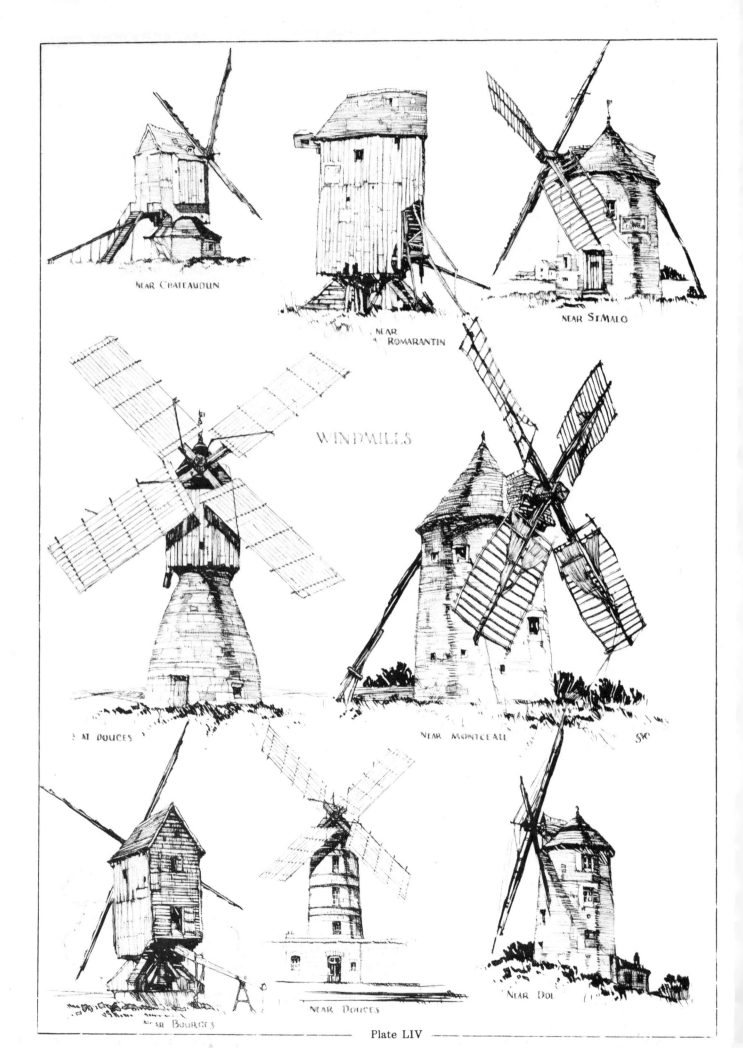

NEAR CHATEAUDUN

NEAR ROMARANTIN

NEAR St MALO

WINDMILLS

AT DOUCES

NEAR MONTCEAU

SVC

NEAR BOURGES

NEAR DOUCES

NEAR DOL

Plate LIV